Light Verse at the End of the Tunnel

Other Books by the Same Author

Snail Morning (Ad Donker)
Doggerel Day (Ad Donker)
Carpe Diem (Carrefour)

GUS FERGUSON

Light Verse at the End
of the Tunnel

POEMS, PROSE & DRAWINGS

Satie wanted to make a theatre for dogs.
The curtain rises. The set consists of a bone.
— Jean Cocteau *(Opium)*

DAVID PHILIP PUBLISHERS
Cape Town Johannesburg

First published 1996 in Southern Africa by David Philip Publishers (Pty) Ltd,
208 Werdmuller Centre, Newry Street, Claremont, 7700 South Africa

ISBN 0 86486 325 X

Some of the items appearing in this collection have already
been published. Acknowledgements are due to the editors of:
ADA, An Alphabet of Small Poems (Sun Belly Press), *Atio,
Blêk-Sem*, the *Cape Times, Carapace, EAR, Femina, Heart in Exile*
(Penguin), *Icarus Rising* (Dye Hard Press), *Imprint, Life Cycle,
Millennium, New Contrast, Noseweek, Odyssey, Scrutiny 2,
Sesame*, the *South African Literary Review, Spectrum*, the *Sunday
Times*, the *Tincture Press* and *Velocipede.*

Typeset by User Friendly
Printed and bound by Forms Xpress, Unit 1, Futura 15, cnr Celie & Bark
Roads, Retreat, 7945 South Africa

Contents

FOR
JO-ANNE FRIEDLANDER
&
TRACEY WALTERS

Weather Report

FORE-WARNED

Knowing from television
That the cold front was coming,
The trees on Signal
Hill, blurred in the mist,
Are more mysterious still.

GALE WARNING

The papaya tree
Flaps in the wind, taps windows
And rattles the eaves:

Flags for the deaf and
Morse for the blind, it signals
With snail-tattered leaves.

Eff the ineffable!

Cosmick Carp

a paradox as parable

Adrift in timeless nothingness –
A darkness sparked with light –
We meet our subject, Cosmick Carp
And recognise his plight.

The Universe it has no sides,
Circumference or rim
But Cosmick's Consciousness of this
Is really rather dim.
His world is vast and boundless,
Lacks limits; is uncurbed
And yet, with all this liberty
Our hero is perturbed.

Although twelve billion trillion miles
He floats with flick of fin:
Infinity describes his cage –
A gaol is what he's in.

He harbours secret fantasies
For tether, stake and lock,
For door and fence and recompense
Of calendar and clock.

But in a way he's just like us
Though freedom is our goal.
We know that Cosmick really wants
A tiny goldfish bowl.

The Metempsychosis of the Yak

He has no house, he has no shack,
Just shaggy hair upon his back
That hangs from cranium to hoof –
An absolutely perfect roof
To shelter him from winter chills
Amongst the Himalayan hills.

Tibetans ride upon the backs
Of generous and gentle yaks
Who offer milk; their hair for rope,
Their flesh for meat, their fat for soap,
And listen as the valley swells
In irony to temple bells

That toll that karmic law decrees
They will return as Red Chinese.

Light Verse at the End of the Tunnel

The perfect poet lies in bed,
In vain he tries to sleep,
He counts and counts inside his head
In syllables, not sheep.

His haiku all have seventeen,
His tankas thirty-one.
His prosody has always been
More regular than Donne.

With fourteen lines and seven rhymes
His sonnets are precise –
How cleverly the music chimes,
How literally nice!

Archaic forms he knows them well:
The ode and virelay,
He likes to write a villanelle
And loves the triolet.

His every pulse is metrical,
Mechanical and neat.
His heart flub-dubs iambical
And never skips a beat.

His ECG scans perfectly
De dum de dum de dum
And measures ineluctably
Each moment's tedium.

His heart's a clock inside a box
That ticks each beat and rhyme
And only Death can spring the lock
To break the spell of time.

But Death does not the poem end
(Of this I can't be surer),
It is, as mystics all contend,
An ultimate caesura.

Laptop poet

Classified Section

Goldfish coming to
Cape Town seeks
bowl in city flat

Midlife Crisis

(or Plato's Cave revisited)

Transfixed, I stand upon the stair
at work and watch, reflected in
the foyer mirror, silhouettes
of children, shadowed on a sun-
bleached wall, careering off to school.

Traders of the Lost Ark

The Waterfront, it has it all –
The mountain-view, the shopping mall,
Boats safely shuffling round the bay,
Jazz, theatre, clubs and cabaret,
Shops, restaurants, pubs and coffee bars
And ample place for parking cars.

And in these high and hallowed halls
The window shopping never palls.
This pleasureland of joyous mood,
This paradise of plenitude
Has buskers, boutiques, doctors' rooms,
Museums too. So one assumes

All needs are met. Yet, things *are* missing
Which just confirms a deep suspicion
That here (like heaven) death's domain
Is always somewhere else. In vain
We search this glorious gala
For signs of church or funeral parlour.

Poetry at the Whale Well

The skeletons of floating whales,
suspended from the roof –
Hindquarters gone completely
from the hip-bone to the hoof.
Their little, ineffectual arms
that dangle at each side
Suggest to us their mothers were
prescribed Thalidomide.

This causes me to speculate,
while poets read their verse,
That Darwin's climb from sea to land
went sometimes in reverse.
Perhaps an ozone crisis let,
in years and years gone by,
Mutational radiation stream
unhindered through the sky

Which sparked a great variety
of new genetic forms
But many species went extinct
or had to shift their norms.
There was a group of herbivores
that stalked the littoral zone –
They were as large as dinosaurs
but mammals to the bone.

And when the cataclysm came,
millennia ago,
These lumbering vegetarians
were dealt a cruel blow –

Their young were born with withered arms,
completely without legs
And lumped around like giant slugs
or rolled about like kegs.

They suffered dehydration sore
beneath the savage sun
Till parents gently nudged them
in the water, one by one.
They flopped and flapped in shallow waves
and found that they could swim –
In ocean as in amnion,
they had no need of limb.

So, buoyant in the surging surf
they mewled their sad goodbyes,
And still today, the sea resounds
with deeply plaintive cries.
This might explain why many die
when stranded by the tide –
Oh, could it be nostalgia drives
the whales' mass suicide?

Before   *After*

Senryu

1
Cycling past
a kiewiet's nest, he stops
to check his chain.

2
The city lights –
a bed of glowing embers.
We dread the kindling wind

3
At the first tremor
it fell from the shelf and broke –
The seismograph.

4
Geography is
everywhere and is, like light,
suddenly gone.

5
A notice in the Cafda bookshop:
Your jigsaw puzzle
is welcome
missing pieces or not.

The Snail Considers Human Worship

Such emphasis on pain and grief!
Self-pitying beyond belief,
Your tears, your wounds and smitten breast
Are both your burden and bequest.

O humankind, how wild you wail.
More put upon than any snail,
Your lamentation rends the air:
'Unfair,' you cry, 'unfair, unfair!'

Be not offended when I say
That nagging God is not the way
To earn angelic wings and harp.
He hates, I'm sure, the way you carp.

Poor souls! There's no epiphany
For those who kyrie: 'Why *me*?'

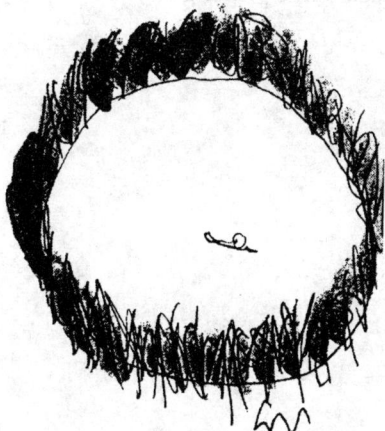

Rhodes Drive Repossession

1

Soon after the zoo closed down
Animals of the small brown
Variety tentatively
But then later less furtively
With goods and chattels, kith and kin
And with a sense of coming home moved in.

2

Freedom, sighed the sage,
Is merely being smaller than
The mesh of the cage.

3

Of course, the zoo we all deplored.
The animals were sorely bored.
We tore it down. And now we've got
An academic parking lot.

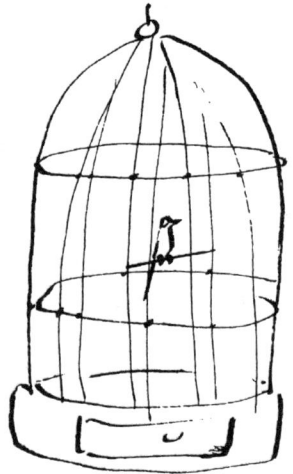

A Eurocentric Sonnet

A fir tree thirty metres high
In silhouette against the sky.
With brush and ink and morning mist
A Chinese watercolourist
Suggests impermanence. But still
Its age and upward striving force
Bears testimony to the will
To live in exile, far from source.

Exotic, alien, displaced,
In southern winds each creaking limb
Longs constantly for wintry wastes
Where pines define the Arctic rim.
Each upturned branch will never know,
Or test, its destined weight of snow.

Finalists – 1996 Haiku World Championships

13

The Bhakti Yogi buys a Bike

For Stephen Daitsh

Astride my dual prayerwheel
I meditate at speed
Devotion to my Dharma is
The only call I heed.

I never lust for victory
Nor crave frenetic motion
But gentle like the Ganges
Flow calmly to the Ocean.

To cycle through the Cosmos is
A karmic task and thrill,
I just adjust my cadence to
The rhythm of each hill.

I have a little mantra that
I murmur on my way
And if you pay attention
You are sure to hear me say:

'Though heavy is the Samsara
And hard to pedal solo;
I do believe Eternity
Is fully Campagnolo.'

Limerick

According to an article printed in The Independent *on 6 July 1994, research into the mating habits of the Praying Mantis, where the female was fed before copulation, proved that no well-fed female ate any of her mates but only one male survived an encounter with a starved female. With apologies to other Skinner/dinner/in her limericks.*

Said a cautious young mantis called Skinner:
I take all of my ladies to dinner.
It's not that I'm kind,
It's just that I find
I feel much more secure when I'm in her.

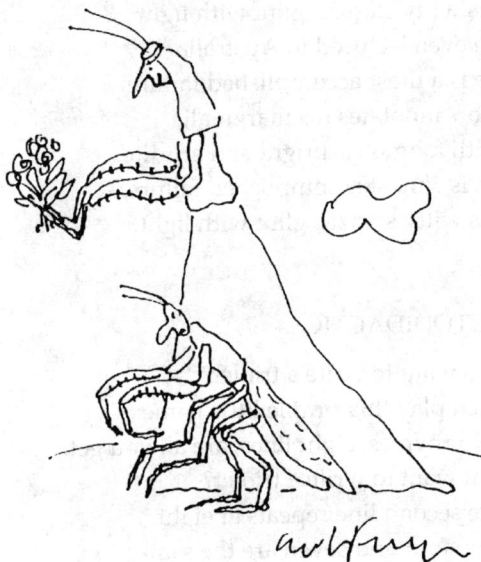

The groom was nervous.

Three Triolets

FOR NICOLETTE

We're driving through the Groot Karoo,
A landscape vast and flat,
You're with me and I'm with you.
We're driving through the Groot Karoo
Which isn't what we planned to do
But this is where we're at –
We're driving through the Groot Karoo,
A landscape vast and flat.

MINOR POET

He is a most accomplished failure,
His witty stanzas glint with light,
He even lectured in Australia.
He is a most accomplished failure
Who annotates his marginalia
With footnotes, bright and erudite.
He is a most accomplished failure,
His witty stanzas glint with light.

AUTODIDACTIC

You want to write a triolet?
Then play this simple little game:
Two rhymes, eight lines, are all you get.
You want to write a triolet?
The second line repeats at eight,
One, four and seven are the same.
You want to write a triolet?
Then play that simple little game.

Cosmick Recreation

Evolutionists and creationists are silly to fight,
As both points of view are essentially right.

Consider a bowl that's thrown just today:
How old, may I ask, how old is the clay?

Open your minds! Unfetter your hearts!
God made the world from second-hand parts.

*Good morning, we are from the Poetry Society, can we come in
and tell you about Hopkins's sprung rhythm?*

Waiting for Bashō

by an ancient pond
a frog sits upon a log
waiting for Bashō

Only One Life He Croaked

'Actually,' he sighed, his knotted
Tongue lolling behind his lips, 'the
Spectrum of my experience
Should be much much broader than yours,
Being amphibian, I am
At home in water and on land.
But the sad truth of the matter
Is a deafeningly humdrum
Diet of flying arthropods
(How I hate the flittering and
Frantic scrabbling in the larynx).
The monotonous perfection
Of this paradisal pond sucks.
My real options are: Bog or log.
Add to all this my morbid
Fear of humans, especially
The large pink ones that wallow
In water and fling stones and (Quel
Horreur!) amputate our long, lithe
Legs to titillate the palate.
Had I options, I would pursue
My private passions – black coffee,
Dragonflywings in aspic, rough
Cognac, Gauloises, the haiku of
Bashō and Issa and, of course,
The paintings of that cubist, Braque.'

Om Mane Padme Hamlet

The Municipality of Middelpad in the Cape announced that, after motivation by its small, but vigorous, Hindu community, all the lampposts in the town are soon to be tuned.

This is to be done by drilling and filing so that when struck by a hard object the hollow poles will reverberate at a pitch conducive to meditation, making each and every lamppost, potentially, a mantric shrine.

The tuning is to be done by Shiva Rampal, a Bengali flautist who hopes to complete the town's eight hundred posts in time for the Hindu Festival of Light.

Delighted with the decision, the leader of the pressure group, Sri Mahalingam van der Poel, said: 'Future plans will include the tuning of wire fences in the surrounding district. Imagine a zephyr melodiously caressing the strings that attempt to demarcate so-called private property. This can only enhance cosmic harmony, social relations and our sense of absurdity.'

The local Dominee, Doctor Joe Grimbeeck, was not opposed to the plans but, as a Christian, felt that tuning to the pitch of church bells would be much more appealing.

Near Wellington

On foot at ten a.m. we saw
hundreds of slimy splotches of
snails who had been, presumably,
traversing the road and were cracked
and splattered by oblivious
wheels of cars. Still, a few survived
sailing serenely on – helmets
skew, feet extended, antennae
moistly probing the morning air.
These, unbidden, with finger and
thumb we airlifted to the grass.

Returning slow and tired at noon
we saw no sign of living snails
crossing the sleeping country road.
The slime, now dry and caked, had merged
with the road's gravel and grey tar.

Back at the farm, after a lunch
of curried vegetables – of herbs,
pumpkin, potato and rhubarb
(a gourmet gastropod's delight)
it suddenly dawned on me while
typing this account that in our
two-hour walk to town and back past
farmland and between twin verges
ticking with life we had not seen
one single, solitary car.

Contact Lenses for Snails

Oscar Glassman, a prominent Sea Point optician and passionate amateur zoologist, was professionally intrigued by the dim-sightedness of the snail.

'If only,' he mused, 'infinitesimal contact lenses could be fashioned to fit the tips of the antennae, what effect might that not have on the lives of the little creepers?' Ruining his own eyes in the process, he worked night after night, with micrometer, grinder and microscope. Twisting his patience to the sharpest point, he made numerous lenses, fitting them gingerly to the feelers of his dim-eyed friends with no apparent success. The snails with optometrically perfect eye caps carried on with no evident change in their sedate slow-motion lives. His friends laughed behind his back. His wife left him for another man who was happy to drink beer with his friends and to tinker in the entrails of renovated cars.

One night, close to tears, his eyes misty with grief, he stood in his garden under the coruscating cosmos. The stars blurred and throbbed in the velvet sky. Suddenly, moved by the terrible beauty of the limitless universe, Glassman's mind made a quantum somersault in his head. On the assumption that snails were short-sighted, he had ground lenses to correct myopia. He now suddenly knew that snails are nocturnal only because they enjoy being ravished by the slow wheeling of the night sky. Snails, he realised are farsighted with telescopic vision. He decided there and then with his failing sight to make lenses to treat hypermetropia.

The new lenses fitted snug as tiny transparent gloves. Their effect was immediate and amazing. Suddenly, after aeons of slow half-blind crawling, insecure, through smudged grass and across bleary earth, the snails, bright with the confidence of the near-sighted, speeded up. Jerking and crashing at first, they soon accelerated their gliding to a hectic 10 kilometres per hour. Scooting across the garden, quick to escape the thrush, the lens-wearing snails took to the blinding day as if millennia of nocturnal crawling were forgotten in the twinkling of a proverbial eye.

This year Glassman was awarded an honorary doctorate in ophthalmology by the University of Cape Town and is tipped as a candidate for a double Nobel prize in zoology and physics. The gentle lens-grinder's constant companion, resembling a fat, furry dachshund, is a seeing-eye mole with glasses.

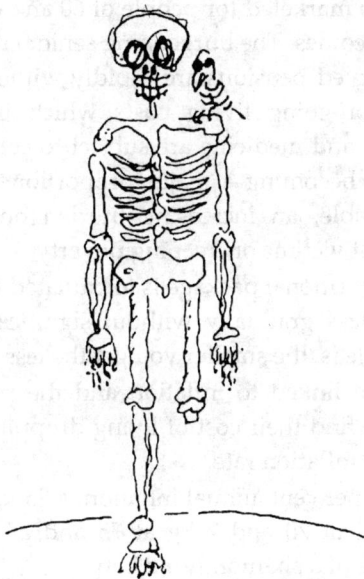

Famous X-Rays 1: Long John Silver

The Elastic Life Formula

Hormones control every aspect of our lives. They hold sway over mood and personality, size, bulk, bone-length, shape, gender and even sexual orientation. When delicate hormonal balances are tampered with, bones lengthen, skin thickens, water is retained and metabolism speeds up or slows down. The human condition is rendered elastic.

With this in mind, coupled with the success of menopausal hormone replacement therapy, the Universal Medical Insurance Group is designing a cost-effective hormone package for the elderly.

The UMIG regimen, tentatively entitled ELF (Elastic Life Formula), is to be marketed for people of 60 and over who are living on fixed incomes. The burgeoning senior citizen tragedy is that well-deserved pensions are rapidly withered by inflation. Whereas, on-going living costs which include food, shelter, transport and medicine are subject to corroding inflation. Seniors are becoming a major proportion of the urban poor, unemployable, an increasing burden on family and State, the innocent victims of creeping poverty.

The ELF polyhormonal package is formulated to reduce human size and mass gradually without significantly altering shape. Its rationale is, the smaller you get the less you need.

Dosage can be linked to inflation and the pensioners on ELF therapy will find their cost of living dropping in indirect proportion to the inflation rate.

Based on a 15 per cent annual inflation, a 75 kg 60-year-old will weigh 15 kg at 70 and 7 kg at 75 and at 80 will have shrunk to the size of a six-month-old baby.

Old-age homes (which will have to be redesigned) will easily accommodate 10 times the number of residents, most of whom will be around 60 cm tall.

Pensioners will be as lovable as pets. Although, on the downside, they could be snatched by cats and birds and if suffering from senile dementia, could easily get lost or trampled underfoot. However, on the upside, endangered seniors could easily hide from burglars and scamper away from muggers.

Childhood perspectives would be restored, facilitating the psychotherapy so necessary for the completion of unfinished business.

Everything will be cheaper. Food, clothing, blankets, transport, make-up and even, ultimately, the coffin and crematorium costs.

For instance, 187 80-year-olds could be packed into a minibus and at least 4 jetsetting geriatrics could snuggle on one aeroplane seat.

60-year-old giants will be seen shambling across retirement village landscapes with dozens of hamster-size nonagenarians peeping from pockets, collars and turn-ups. One banana will feed a dozen, a bottle of beer could fire a bacchanalian orgy and a pocket handkerchief would do as a tablecloth, tent or tarpaulin.

What is still unpredictable is the long-term effect of ELF on longevity. Trials using rats, indicate that side-effects might be uncontrolled promiscuity and premature ageing.

Bonzai Rain Forests – near Knysna

An Alphabet of Small Poems

AUTOPHAGY

Amongst cannibals
The phrase "battered wife" assumes
Another meaning.

BURNS'S HAIKU
from Tam o'Shanter – for Stewart Conn

… like the snow falls in
the river, a moment white –
then gone forever.

CREDO

I know for sure one thing that's true:
The Universe is just a clue.

DYSEXLIC

She signs her letter:
'Lost and lost of love.'

EPIGRAM
Source: Patricia Davison

Lost in the hills at the end of day
We burned the map to light the way.

FREE FALL

The Woman's Movement
Began, I believe,
With Adamant Eve.

GRENADE

What a condition to find ourselves in:
With just enough strength to pull out the pin
But not, I'm afraid, to throw the grenade.

HAIKU

The five, seven, five,
Seventeen syllable form
Has stunted my style!

INTERNET SENRYU

I believe that G-d
Encrypted the Universe
For fear of hackers.

JUSTIFICATION

Life is but a gift of time
Spent in gathering evidence
Against the summons for the crime
Of wasting that inheritance.

KITE

Victorious kite
Aloft in the wild weather,
You are, without doubt,
At the end of your tether.

LIGHT VERSE

The sun that rolls across the sky
Is massive, dense and round
Yet casts quite paradoxically
No shade upon the ground.

MAYA

Awake this morning
and all I see is Buddha –
Marvellous Maya!

NEMESIS

Barefoot in the city street
Holding fate to scorn
I picked my way through glinting glass
And trampled on a thorn.

OLD AGE

Your life-support system
Is coin-operated.
The Matron has change.

POET

Desperate for praise:
He quotes rejection slips.

QUO VADIS

The oceans that are so abused
By mercantile and plunderous hand
Surround, and are contained by land.

ROMANTIC POET

He reads with feeling.
It's not appealing.

SELF PITY

My life in action replay:
Fifty perfect goals
And me the goalie.

THIEVES
Source: Matthew aged 2

They came in the dark,
Took the mountain away
And left only mist.

UTOPIA

If dogs did bark and birds did fly,
Were blue the hue of cloudless sky,
If bells did ring and starlings sing,
The world would be a perfect thing.

VOWEL MOVEMENT

Defecation
Scatology
Deification
Eschatology

WORLD WITHOUT END
On the death of an old computer

Dos to Dos
Ascii to Ascii

XHAIKU

Amaxoxo
ayangxola ngokuba
afuna uxolo!

Bullfrogs / make a noise because / they are demanding peace.

YULE

It's the end of the World:
Sales at Christmas and
A begging Santa Claus.

ZOSHI SAID

The Piet-My-Vrou
Talks Afrikaans,
Don't you know?

The Final Album: Life support – unplugged

A Ballistic Bulletin

A snail, learning English, was most impressed
To find the word 'shell' with two meanings blest.

'Ironical,' he remarked with a smile
'To mean both protection and projectile!'

'So what,' sighed his shell-less pal with a shrug,
'Just think of the ponderous pun on "slug"!'

Bookseller

1995
You know that poetry doesn't sell
Especially new or local stuff.
I should say no but, what the hell!
Give me two. No, one's enough.

2000
The book you're holding in your hand
Just shows your erudition.
A bargain at nine hundred rand –
That is a first edition.

Puritan against the Wind

for Lee Fox

When every pedal stroke's a bore
When bum and back and neck are sore
And flesh is mortified for sure,
Then, I believe, my soul will soar.

Willow on Prozac

Vulture

As the 20th century stumbles towards its apocalyptic close, everything, it seems, has become problematic. Even high-flown concepts like nature conservation have their sinister aspect.

Diligently maintained and well-stocked game parks juxtaposed with rural poverty brings privilege and deprivation cheek by rasping jowl, with the implication that nature conservation is at the expense of mankind.

While this view might be muddleheaded and infinitely debatable, what is clear is that synergistic solutions are wanted if we are to turn the tanker back towards Eden and save the world.

Take the sad case of *Gyps coprotheres*, the Cape Vulture. Until recently the vulture, like the hyena, was viewed with total disgust. Dismissed as scavenger, gobbler of carrion and devourer of filth – this innocent and useful necrophiliac was considered obscene; evolved to squabble, bicker and scuffle over the remains of noble and beautiful creatures. Greedy necks and slobbering beaks thrusting into rotting carcasses was a scene that only a Baudelaire could extol as beautiful.

But we have had a paradigm shift. The planet is one huge, delicately balanced eco-system. Conservation is cool. Animals are wonderful and, as always, only man is vile. Even vultures are OK. Transcendental in flight, their earth-bound lurch and hobble is now seen to be comical and they are definitely part of some essential food-chain and are, above all, an endangered species.

Their endangerment is simply due to the dearth of appropriate nourishment. Game and livestock have become, thanks to human greed, too commercially valuable to be allowed to die, as they were designed to, in the veld. The spiral of moribund meandering mimicked by the swirl of birds in the implacable sky.

So-called wild animals are now almost totally incarcerated, colonised and exploited as tourist attractions.

Today, many vultures, who need animal bone to build their aerodynamic fames, live and die flightless as the dodo due to a lack of calcium in their diet. That is, if they don't choke to death on gladwrap from discarded braaipacks.

Not that the vultures do not have champions. We hear that one saintly member of a recently formed vulture support group is leaving money in his will to ensure that his corpse will be ceremoniously placed in vulture country high in the Magaliesberg.

This extraordinary person (a Prometheus in reverse) has also, on occasion, lain dead still for hours (dreaming, no doubt, of the soft beat of angel wings) under the indifferent gaze of several drifting birds. Unsuccessful attempts at interspecies hara kiri.

As much as we can admire the foregoing, one Sydney Cartonesque gesture is not enough. What is called for is organisation and infrastructure.

We need to institute a South African version of the Parsee way of death. Orthodox Parsees, followers of Zoroaster, have a funerary rite which calls for the laying of the corpse, three days after death, when the soul has departed, on a 'tower of silence' so that it can be consumed by vultures and other birds of prey.

Although for the Parsees, this method of corporeal dissolution is to prevent the defilement of earth, water or fire, in our case it would be an act of conservation and charity towards an endangered species, a saving of graveyard real estate and a practical step towards interspecies amity.

It also means that flesh as well as spirit will be lifted up in flight.

Cape Town has thousands of suitably flat-topped buildings that could be used as towers of silence on a roster or permanent basis. Mordeaux Mansions in Sea Point might be chosen as a 'tower of the month' for July and be mournfully draped with crepe and hung with limply flapping flags.

But, since not only vultures gain from the death of a loved one, status and snobbery will most likely creep in. Probably the more expensive the funeral the more prestigious the tower. The poor will be carelessly dumped onto the roof of our lacklustre Civic Centre while the well-to-do might make it to the top of the Cape Sun or yuppies could be placed on the roof of the Waterfront Mall.

The possibilities are endless. But one thing is sure – our skies will again be alive with the rush of vulturine wings and wild, excited croaking. Conservation at the expense of mankind will take on a new meaning.

LOVE AMONGST THE MIDDLE-AGED

Sleeping-Mates

A 1995 survey of more than 5 000 frequent flyers revealed some startling facts and has led to the development of a fascinating new travel service. 72 per cent of the travellers interviewed by Marketpro were males aged between 40-60, mainly in middle and upper management, who were away from home between 3-6 days per month.

The survey further showed that by far the majority were heterosexual and married or in stable, more or less monogamous relationships. A parallel probe by the marketing company of escort agencies and massage parlours in major cities indicated similar opinion. Most of the clients were middle-aged and most were on business trips. Information on their marital status was, for some reason, unreliable.

On investigating individual cases using psychologists, it was discovered that the majority of the clients were not seeking sex but comfort.

Three nights away from home was reported to be unsettling. Despite the luxury of the hotel rooms, sleep was shallow and disturbed. Also, many of the interviewees had bad or worrisome dreams. Post-Business-Trip-Trauma studies revealed alarming increase in paranoia and acute depression.

As a result of this research the hotel group that commissioned the survey has just introduced a pilot programme called Sleeping-Mate. The service is offered discreetly to business men who can, for an additional fee billed as extra room service, hire a middle-aged woman who comes with a full kit of flannel nightie, comfortable pillows, Horlicks and fluffy slippers.

Sex is not offered as an option and so far in the pilot study has never even been negotiated. Results have been phenomenally interesting.

The businessmen report tremendous mood elevation causing mild euphoria during business meetings and sharper concentration.

An advertisement in an evening newspaper which ran for a week offering the service in Johannesburg had 950 enquiring callers of which 790 were more than interested and were even prepared to leave call-back numbers.

The businessmen who have used the service already seem delighted. They're less miserable on business trips and those that have previously gone to escorts feel far less guilty; many of them have reported enthusiastically to their wives on the therapeutic benefits of this service.

In fact, a leading Cape Town corporate attorney has become so friendly with his regular sleeping-mate, a 52-year-old recently retrenched legal secretary, that he has invited her to Cape Town for a holiday to meet his wife and family.

Another advertisement tentatively seeking applications for the position of sleeping-mates has had an enormous response from middle-aged women from all walks of life, many of whom live quite lonely lives following divorce or demise of their husbands. For instance, a not untypical applicant Sonia, who is 61, has a repertoire of eighty-three fairy stories and is a retired investment consultant with a diploma in aromatherapy.

The phenomenon being marketed is not new. In Roman times it was common for householders to rent out their houses and wives to travellers while they themselves took a few days off visiting wine houses. Not to mention also the tradition of chamber maids that disappeared in our puritanical century.

The MD of the hotel group said in an interview that the promotion was not meant to be genderist in any way, the focus on heterosexual couples was purely the result of the opportunity presented by the survey. The needs of women and non-heterosexual travellers are also being addressed.

When the pilot study is complete the product will be fully marketed, offering corporate discounts and a link to Voyager miles.

I refuse to get into bed until you've tidied the room.

Sonnet in Couplets

Though time exacts its normal tax
This lovely lady can relax.
She has no need of nip and tuck
Nor fears the dreaded liposuck.

He watches her across the room.
Her radiance dispels the gloom
As moon, perceived by fading eye,
Is softly blurred against the sky.

In waning light and warmer tones
Erogenous nocturnal zones
Respond to touch unseen by sight.
If love is blind then, welcome night!

Her lover's love remains emphatic –
He's mercifully astigmatic.

He buys me roses, not for love but out of pity for the vendors!

Love amongst the Middle-aged

For Nicky after 11323 blissful mornings

Each morn at dawn the slanting light,
Romantic in my failing sight,
Surrounds, like love, her perfect form.

She moves about our nuptial dorm
And murmurs as in deep despair;
'Whatever is a girl to wear?'

I watch with tea cup in my grip,
Its rim obscures my trembling lip,
And realise how much I'm blessed:

Awakening from a long night's rest
To witness, freed from lust's blind curse,
My daily striptease in reverse.

St Agatha in the grass